Leadership
Haiku

Increasing Your Impact And Influence
17 Syllables At A Time

BARRY ZWEIBEL

LeadershipTraction®
847-291-9735 | info@leadershiptraction.com
www.leadershiptraction.com

Cover Design: Anthony Morrison

ISBN-13: 978-0-9722130-5-9
(LeadershipTraction Press)

ISBN-10: 0-9722130-5-8

DEDICATION

To Nancy, My Wife.
My Buddy. My Pal. My Chum.
I'll Love You, Always.

CONTENTS

ACKNOWLEDGEMENTS

Leadership Haiku evolved, in large part, from the influence of two people – one I know quite well, and one I do not.

The first is my son (and technology mentor), Andy.

So many years ago, Andy suggested I start using Twitter. "It's the next logical step for you and your business, Dad," he said. "You should give it a try."

Initially, I found it quite difficult to capture meaningful thoughts in 140 characters, or less. It was so much easier (and more enjoyable) to just respond to whatever other people were tweeting about. So I did what any struggling Twitter newbie, and avid Chicago Cubs baseball fan, would do – I began following the "#Cubs" hashtag while watching the games on TV.

Enter Ed Nickow.

A diehard Cubs fan, and active twitterer, Ed was tweeting all of his in-game play-by-play, commentary, and related musings as 17-syllable, haiku poems!

"That's brilliant!" I thought. "Blue Ocean brilliant!"

(For those not familiar with the *Blue Ocean Strategy*, it's a method for creating *'oceans'* of opportunity by taking recognized, but typically never-before connected activities and combining them in unique and appealing new ways. (Think *Cirque du Soleil* with its blend of ballet, theatre, gymnastics, and the circus. Or Southwest Airlines and its low fares, "bags fly free," no change fees, and ultra-friendly staff. Or the way that Ed was tweeting his clever missives about his favorite baseball team and their goings-on.)

Well, it didn't take long before I was counting syllables and tweeting out my own "#Cubs" haiku, which Ed, Andy, and others kindly retweeted.

Rooting for a losing team was never such fun!

But Andy's purported "next logical step" really took form once I realized I could also be tweeting my leadership development messages in haiku-format.

And *Leadership Haiku* was born.

So thank you, Andy. And thank you, Ed. Thanks, too, to my wife, Nancy; daughter, Jessie; mom, 'Seets'; Joe 'Spud' Contrera; Donna 'Peachy' Brown; Therese Gustafson; Ed Rudick; Doug Wiseman; 'Leeesa' Kemp; Cinnie Noble; Mark Ellwood; Helen Yin; Dave and Viv Fantauzzi; Sally Zepeda; Cynthia Roby; Nancy Woehr; Anthony Morrison; LeRae Gidyk; Bernie Richie; Jim Carlini; Vicki Raymont; Jackie Yun; John Bernard; Leigh Henderson; Jeffery J. Fox; and Tim Dant. You each played a part in helping this book become a reality. I'll be forever grateful.

Barry Zweibel
Chicagoland, 2015

INTRODUCTION

As a leader, you're likely already familiar with, and at least somewhat proficient in, one or more of the four directional domains of exemplary leadership: *Managing Up, Managing Down, Managing Across,* and *Managing Within.*

Managing Up refers to your ability to create and maintain effective working relationships with your boss, more senior executives, board members, company stakeholders, and influencers.

How can you tell if you're not *Managing Up* as effectively as you might? If your boss is not deferring to your judgment as much as you'd like, not supporting you when you need it most, not sufficiently advocating on your behalf, not asking for your opinion before key decisions are made, not assigning you to high-profile projects or hot-hot priorities, or not giving you the raises, bonuses, or recognition you think you deserve, those are all indicators that your *Managing Up* skills are wanting.

Managing Up is most *under-utilized* direction in which to lead because of how many people feel they shouldn't have to manage up. So they don't.

Hopefully, you're not making this same mistake. But if you are, or are looking for ways to do a better job in this leadership domain, then you'll want to pay particular attention to what's in Chapter 1.

Managing Down, the most consistently *thought of* direction in which to lead, refers to your ability to create and maintain effective working relationships with direct reports, company operatives, and support staff directly or indirectly affiliated with your operation.

You can tell if you're *Managing Down* effectively because you'll see particularly high levels of employee morale, retention, productivity, creativity, teamwork, cooperation, and professionalism.

The opposite of that, coupled with increasing levels of employee stress and strain, whining, absenteeism (especially on Mondays and Fridays), extended coffee breaks, cliquishness, missed deadlines, ignored commitments, and eroding trust and loyalty, all likely indicate your *Managing Down* skills could benefit from some serious improving. If that's the case, you'll find Chapter 2 to be particularly worthwhile.

Managing Across refers to your ability to create and maintain effective working relationships with peers and those internal (in other parts of your organization) and external (your vendor contacts, customers, and other industry colleagues and professionals).

Managing Across is considered the most *discounted* direction in which to lead, which is a shame — especially when you consider that, if you're like most leaders, pretty much everything you try to accomplish requires lateral support and horizontal collaboration.

In the absence of *Managing Across*, you'll likely notice that group decision-making falters, important initiatives lose traction, camaraderie, partnership, and teamwork are supplanted by politicking, passive- or openly-aggressive behaviors and one-upmanship – and that meetings, elevator rides, and even benign hallway interactions are becoming increasingly awkward, annoying, and counterproductive.

Chapter 3 explores *Managing Across*, and eliminating its dysfunctional byproducts, in more detail.

So those are three of the four directional domains of exceptional leadership. But to be truly successful, leaders must attend to the most-important fourth domain, as well: *Managing Within*.

Unquestionably, the most *challenging* direction in which to lead, *Managing Within* refers to your ability to create and maintain effective relationships with *yourself*. That is, how your thoughts, feelings, beliefs, and attitudes directly and indirectly affect the decisions you make, and the behaviors you model – especially when you're stressed.

Not recognizing your impact and/or not taking responsibility for it, are primary indicators of a need to upgrade your *Managing Within* skillset.

Chapter 4 looks at ways you can do that, quickly, easily, and in many cases, almost effortlessly.

WHY HAIKU ABOUT LEADERSHIP?

The haiku is a form of ancient Japanese poetry designed to evoke a lasting thought, feeling, or impression from just (and only) 17 phonetic syllables, or '音' (pronounced 'on') using a 5/7/5 pattern across three non-rhyming lines. (The word 'haiku' is singular *and* plural, like 'moose,' 'salmon,' or 'series.')

Originally inspired by the beauty of nature and the changing of seasons, haiku subject-matter has broadened considerably through the ages. Now using haiku for leadership development tutorials expands the form even further.

But it's totally logical. Haiku provide quick, energizing, bursts of insight and inspiration. They afford natural pauses for reflection. They're short enough to be read in a single breath — even *you* have time for that! They offer increased nuance and meaning with each subsequent reread. And, they have a crisp, minimalist aesthetic, giving them a very modern feel.

Need a quick refresh or recharge? There's a haiku for that! Not sure how to handle a tricky situation? There's a haiku for that, too! *A Leadership Haiku!*

Most Learning Takes Time,
A Surprising Amount, Though,
Takes But A Haiku!

HOW TO USE THIS BOOK

It is not necessary to read this book from front to back or cover to cover. While you're invited to start at the beginning and read straight through, you can also just open it up to any page and dig right in.

It's entirely your choice.

That said, *Leadership Haiku* IS meant to be read repeatedly — like a favorite affirmation, inspirational message, or winning lottery ticket you just purchased.

It's also recommended that you reread it quarterly to better notice how different haiku catch your attention at different times — that's a meaningful indicator of your growth and development as a leader.

Leadership Haiku is also intended to be read *interactively.* So highlight, underline, dog-ear, and bookmark its pages; write notes in the margins and on the blank pages at the back; and use different colored pens and markers as you go, so you can easily see which haiku stood out for you the last time you read it. And the times before that.

Also, keep *Leadership Haiku* handy, where you can easily see it and refer to it at work. Let it serve as a daily reminder of how important it is for you to become the best leader you possibly can.

If you travel for business, you may want to put an extra copy in your briefcase. Airport delays are inevitable, but with a copy of *Leadership Haiku*, in hand, time will fly by — whether you're reading it quietly, by yourself, or using it as a conversation-starter with someone sitting next to you.

And since most people learn best through conversation, why not really get things going by sharing your favorite haiku (and the ones that give you pause) with friends, family members, colleagues, and those you coach and mentor? You can also explore them with those who coach and mentor you.

While you're at it, why not place a few copies out in your reception area for visitors to browse and enjoy? Maybe they're a bit early; maybe you're running a little late. Regardless, it's a nice way to shift attention away from the waiting and onto them wanting to chat about *their* favorite haiku.

Then there's giving copies of *Leadership Haiku* to others as gifts. It's a unique, memorable, and business-appropriate way to say thank you or congratulations, *and* stimulate some interesting dialogue about what exemplary leaders do.

In using this book in these ways, you'll not only be increasing your own impact and influence, you'll be helping others to actively accelerate their leadership development, as well — 17-syllables at a time!

Welcome to *Leadership Haiku!*

Leadership Haiku

Increasing Your Impact And Influence
17 Syllables At A Time

BARRY ZWEIBEL

MANAGING UP

1.

Managing Your Boss
Is Not The Entire Story,
But It's A Large Part.

2.

How Do You Stand Out?
Is It By The Good You Do?
Or Your Excuses?

3.

Listen For What's Said.
Listen For What Is Not Said.
Compare And Contrast.

4.

Success Breeds Success.
Failure Breeds Success, Too,
If It's Handled Well.

5.

To Have An Impact
Your Words Must Say Something New
Not Rehash The Old.

6.

When Problems Are Few
The Value-Added You Bring
Must Intensify.

7.

At Least Once A Month
Review Your Goals For The Year.
Keep Them Top-Of-Mind.

8.

How Adept Are You
At Not Being Surprised By
What You're Surprised By?

9.

A Leader Insures
Important Information
Always Flows Upstream.

10.

Ambiguity
Is Just Another Word For
"Go Figure It Out."

11.

When You Influence,
What Do You Do That You Don't,
Whenever You Don't?

12.

Sometimes You May Want
To Pretend You Know Something.
Try To Fight That Urge.

13.

Good News Or Bad News,
When Sharing Information,
Make Sure It's *New* News.

14.

Sometimes, The Worst News
Provides Opportunities
The Best News Cannot.

15.

Feedback Not So Good?
But If That's What They're Thinking
It's Better You Know.

16.

When Working a Task
Do You Play At The Edges?
Or Hit It Head On?

17.

Respond To Questions
Both Crisply And Succinctly.
And Don't Bend The Truth.

18.

Anticipating
And Acting Accordingly.
THAT Is Leadership.

19.

Check Your Assertions.
Are They *Truly* True, Or Just
What You *Want* To Be?

20.

Do You Influence?
Consider How You Express
Your Key Messages.

21.

What Creates Value
Is Not Just What You Achieve,
But In What Context.

22.

Bad News Is Bad News.
But It's Much Better News Than
Bad News You Withhold.

23.

Asking For Advice
Is *Not* A Sign Of Weakness.
There's Strength In Learning.

24.

Meeting With The Boss.
A Faster Tempo Needed.
Cleaner, Crisper...Go!

25.

Just Getting Noticed
Is Not A Substitute For
Notice-Worthiness.

26.

The Questions You're Asked
And The Answers You Provide
Should Always Align.

27.

Rework Your Message.
Focus Less On What You'll Say;
More On What They'll Hear.

28.

Difficult Choices
Define A Leader's Success
More Than Correct Ones.

29.

Never Be So Proud
That You Can't Ask The Question,
"Can You Help Me, Please?"

30.

That Special Project
Your Boss Assigned You Today...
That Is Your *Real* Job.

31.

Ask For What You Need.
And Ask For What You Want, Too.
Just Know Which Is Which.

32.

Big Meeting Today.
Time To Get Ready: Over.
Time To Impress: Now.

33.

It's Not What You Know
As Much As It's What You Do
When You Do Not Know.

34.

Flexibility:
The Ability To Change
Without Much Ado.

35.

Show Your Character.
Do The Right Thing Even If
It's The Harder Choice.

36.

Sometimes Perceptions
Can Have Way More Sway Than Facts.
Act Accordingly.

37.

That Your Boss Is Tough
Is Really Not Relevant.
You Can Be Tough, Too.

38.

A Failure To Plan
Is The Most Common Reason
Executives Fail.

39.

Getting Approval
Requires Not Just Good Ideas
But Good Rationale.

40.

What Is Your Value?
What Are You Really Good At?
Go Do More Of That.

41.

What Would Be Helpful
For Your Boss To Tell Your Staff?
Have Your Boss Say That.

42.

When Suggesting Risk
Always Explain Your Plans For
Mitigating It.

43.

A Crisply Worded
Executive Summary
Helps Bosses Say "Yes!"

44.

Sometimes Leadership
Is More About Readiness
Than About Doing.

45.

Sometimes Success Is
About Quickly Fixing Things.
So Fix Things Quickly.

46.

When Crises Occur
Leaders Accept The Pressure
And Do Their Best Work.

47.

You May Be An Expert
But There Still Is Much To Learn.
Be Open To That.

48.

Elevator Shuts.
Just You And Your Boss' Boss.
Ready To Engage?

49.

What Marquee Projects
Are You Managing Right Now?
If None, Volunteer.

50.

Opportunities
Often Appear First As Threats.
Don't Get Defensive.

51.

How You Spend Your Time
Highlights Your Priorities
As What They Are Not.

52.

Who Takes Your Phone Calls
Is A Good Indicator
Of Your Influence.

53.

Anticipating
The Unanticipated.
THAT Is Leadership.

54.

Poise Under Pressure:
You, Responding To Questions,
Mess Notwithstanding.

55.

'Either/Or' Thinking
Rarely Solves Complex Problems.
But, 'And' Thinking Can.

56.

Avoidance Of Blame
Can Cause More Blameworthiness
Than Accepting Blame.

57.

What Tends To Happen
When You're Not Fully Prepared
Is Avoidable.

58.

Help Your Boss Hear You.
What's Your Headline? What's Your Point?
Always Start With That.

59.

Just Doing Your Job
Won't Get You A Great Review.
More's Needed Than That.

60.

What Does Your Boss Need
To Support Your Decisions
More Consistently?

61.

Your Boss Needs Candor.
Not Complaints, Gripes, Or Whining.
Choose Your Words And Tone.

62.

'Constructive Feedback'
Is NOT Something To Avoid.
Embrace It, Fully.

63.

When Asked A Question
Prove You Were Listening By
Answering Crisply.

64.

Don't Forget To Get
All The Info That You Need
To Know What You Need.

65.

Articulate The
Business Justification.
Early And Often.

66.

One Part What You Say
And Three Parts How You Say It.
That's *Managing Up!*

67.

Create Advocates
By Going The Extra Mile
When You Don't Have To.

68.

When Aggravated
Don't React From Emotion.
Respond With Logic.

69.

How Right You Might Be
Is Only As Relevant
As How Right You Are.

70.

A Line Must Be Drawn
Between Patiently Waiting
And Being Ignored.

71.

Build Relationships
By Making It Easier
To Know You Better.

72.

Conflict Gets Harder
When You Focus More On *You*
Than You Do On *It*.

73.

Don't Assume Intent.
Behaviors Often Mislead.
Always Verify.

74.

How Do You Gather
Intel On What's Going On?
Hopefully, Often.

75.

Take Others' Ideas
Two, Or Three Steps Further.
Be A Thought Leader.

76.

What Frightens You Most?
What Takes You Out Of Your Game?
Discuss, Privately.

77.

The Problem Is Clear.
The Solution Is Less So.
Good Thing You're Involved.

78.

What Is Engagement?
Accepting The Lunacy
Cuz You Like The Work.

79.

What's Your BIG Idea?
What Would Your Boss Say It Is?
'Branding' Does Matter.

80.

When Asking Questions
You Can Encourage Candor
By Being Polite.

81.

If You're Always 'On'
Your Boss Will Start Wondering
If You're Really Real.

82.

Pressure Makes Leaders.
Carbon Morphed Into Diamonds.
Are You In Or Out?

83.

Don't Ignore Emails.
Why Show The Big Boss You Can't
Manage Your Workload?

84.

Manipulation:
The Dark-Side of Influence.
Know Where The Line Is.

85.

Success Over *There*
Won't Guarantee Success *Here,*
But It Often Helps.

86.

Stop Kidding Yourself.
Just Because You Think You're Right,
Doesn't Mean You Are.

87.

What Needs To Be Said
Really Does Need To Be Said.
And *You* Should Say It.

88.

Whenever Confused
Don't Pretend You're Keeping Up.
That Rarely Works Well.

89.

Cooperation:
The Act Of Overlooking
Whatever Annoys.

90.

As The Tensions Mount,
Remember That Days Like These
Are Why You Get Paid!

91.

In Its Simplest Form
Accountability
Encourages Growth.

92.

It's What You Do With
The Things You *Don't* Want To Do
That Tells Your Story.

93.

No Matter How Bad
Your Yesterday Might Have Been,
Today Matters More.

94.

Where Did You Leave Things?
What Might Have Happened If You
Went A Bit Further?

95.

When It's Time, It's Time.
Some Things Should Not Be Delayed.
So Do Not Delay.

96.

What Are You Doing?
What Are You Doing Right Now?
How *Should* You Answer?

97.

The Patterns Are There.
They're Just Not Apparent, Yet.
Focus And You'll See.

98.

What's Aggravating?
Why Is It Triggering You?
The Mirror Tells All.

99.

So Many Headaches
Can Be Mitigated By
Acting More Quickly.

100.

You Don't Need More Time.
You Just Need To Learn How To
Do With Less Of It.

MANAGING DOWN

101.

The Warmth Of A Smile.
The Tone Of A Few Kind Words.
Loyalty Takes Shape.

102.

What You Say, Matters.
What You Don't Say Matters, Too.
Those Are Your Options.

103.

Delegate Sooner.
Waiting Rarely Improves Things
And Wastes Precious Time.

104.

By Definition
Only One Priority
Can Be #1.

105.

When Deadlines Are Missed
Holding Staff Accountable
Does Not Make You Bad.

106.

Mood And *Energy.*
Two Great Indicators Of
Engagement...Or Not.

107.

Don't Shy Away From
Difficult Conversations.
They're Too Important.

108.

Go Tell Your Staff How
To Get The Most Out Of You.
Help Everyone Win.

109.

To Be A Great Boss
You Have To WANT To Be One.
It All Starts Right There.

110.

Alter Your Approach.
Not To Be Inconsistent
But To Test Ideas.

111.

Done, But Not Finished.
Key Elements Still Missing.
Time To Teach Them Why.

112.

How Are You Helping
The People Who Work For You
To Listen Better?

113.

If Staff Knows That You
Respect Them And What They Say,
They'll Tell You A Lot.

114.

Learn Something Today
And Then Teach It Tomorrow.
THAT Is Leadership.

115.

You Know The Things That
Lousy Bosses Tend To Do?
Do The Opposite!

116.

Want To Show That You're
A Leader Worth Following?
Ask Better Questions.

117.

Delegation Is
Decision-Making *For* You
Instead Of *By* You.

118.

Be Sure To Tell Them
Not Just *When* Their Work Is Due
But *How* You'll Use It.

119.

How Engaged Are You
In Engaging Employees
To Be More Engaged?

120.

When Staff Works Harder
Even When You're Not Around.
THAT is Leadership.

121.

When Your Staff Screws-Up
They'll Give You Their Attention.
So Say Something Smart.

122.

When Problems Arise
Your Initial Reactions
Empower, Or Not.

123.

You Know What To Do.
But That's Really Not The Point.
Let THEM Run With It.

124.

Do You Act The Same
When You Think No One's Watching?
They're *Always* Watching!

125.

Give Your Staff Choices.
Learn Just How Good They Are At
Making Decisions.

126.

So Many Problems
Are Caused Inadvertently.
Notice Your Impact.

127.

Does Timing Matter?
Change An Assignment After
They're Finished...And See.

128.

How Frantic Are You?
As In Really, How Frantic?
Dial That Down A Bit!

129.

Ever Stop To Think
That The Tone You Use
Is What They'll Recall?

130.

Leaders Delegate
As Soon As It's Possible.
Not After A While.

131.

Are You A Mentor?
Do You Share Your Lessons Learned?
If Not, Then Why Not?

132.

How Well Do You Know
The People That You Work With?
Take Time To Find Out.

133.

People Can Be Great
If You Ask Them To Be Great.
Ask Them To Be Great.

134.

Do You Clarify?
Or Just Further Complicate?
What Would Others Say?

135.

Staff Missing Deadlines?
Explain How Your Work Can't Start
'Til They Finish Theirs.

136.

Create True Moments
With Everyone You Work With.
It Helps Morale Soar.

137.

It Is Your Job To
Create A Compelling View
Of How Things Could Be.

138.

Take A Look Around.
Who's Not Paying Attention?
What Will Engage Them?

139.

Your Best Employees
Appreciate A Challenge.
Don't Make Them Ask Twice.

140.

Don't Give Year-End Goals.
Make Them Due *Throughout* The Year.
That Helps Get More Done.

141.

Ending Your Meetings
5 To 10 Minutes Early.
THAT Is Leadership.

142.

When A Missed Deadline
Is Accepted As The Norm
Commitment Dwindles.

143.

Answering Questions
Isn't Your Primary Job.
Asking Questions Is.

144.

Attentive Leaders
Look Things Over Rather Than
Overlooking Them.

145.

Do You Listen Well?
Go Ask Someone To Tell You
What You *Didn't* Hear!

146.

How Polite Are You?
Treat Others Respectfully
Regardless Of Rank.

147.

Some Conversations
Start Without Any Problem.
Others Need Prompting.

148.

Sometimes, It's Just Noise.
Other Times, More Substantive.
Be Sure What Matters.

149.

Some Things Can't Be Rushed.
Other Things Certainly Can.
Hmmm, Now Which Is Which?!

150.

Some Staff Dive Right In.
Some Wait To Be Invited.
Remember Them, Too.

151.

The Best Way To Learn?
Asking Meaningful Questions.
Best Way To Teach? Same!

152.

What's The Objective?
How Will It Benefit Us?
Build A Shared Vision.

153.

The Heat Of Summer
Is Not As Oppressive As
A Lousy Leader.

154.

Wandering Around
May Not Seem So Strategic,
But It Really Is.

155.

When A Leader Speaks,
What Is Said Matters, Plenty.
But *How*, Even More.

156.

Your Reputation
Is Defined By What You Do
And What You Don't Do.

157.

Wishing And Hoping
For Something Good To Happen
Is Not Your Best Move.

158.

Helping Them Focus
On The *Right* Priorities.
THAT Is Leadership.

159.

What Motivates *You*
May Not Be The Same As What
Motivates Your Staff.

160.

What Are They Saying?
Keep An Ear To The Grapevine.
Don't Just Think You Know.

161.

Some Weeks Go So Fast
While Others Go So Slowly.
Just Like...Employees!

162.

Busy As You Are
Still Share A Kind Word With Staff
As You Hurry By

163.

Focused People Are
Much More Productive People.
Help Them Focus More.

164.

People Like To Be
A Part Of Something Bigger.
Leaders Will Let Them.

165.

How Aligned Are The
Opinion Leaders On Staff
With Your Perspectives?

166.

Great! You're Doing Great!
Now What Will It Take To Make
Great Even *More* Great?!

167.

Oftentimes More Time
Does Not Improve One's Results.
Deadlines Prevent Waste.

168.

When You Do Not Know
And Can Admit It When Asked,
THAT Is Leadership.

169.

What You Think Matters
May Matter, But Don't Ignore
What They Think Matters.

170.

When Tensions Run High
What Do You Do To Help Staff
Better Cope With Stress?

171.

Always Check Your Tone
So That It Doesn't Belie
What You Are Saying.

172.

Consensus-Building
Without "Because I Say So."
Go Deeper Than That.

173.

What Does Your Staff Do
That You Want To See More Of?
What About Less Of?

174.

Inspiring Others
Is What Leaders Tend To Do
When Being Themselves.

175.

Leaders Are Good At
Getting The 'Quiet' People
To Speak Up, As Well.

176.

Being Respectful
Develops Relationships
And Lessens Distrust.

177.

When Leaders Listen
It Makes A Real Difference.
So, Too, When They Don't.

178.

Job One For A Boss
Is Not To *Be* The Expert,
But To *Grow* Experts.

179.

Knowing When To Push.
Knowing When To Pull, Instead.
THAT Is Leadership.

180.

Deadline Approaching.
Status Of Things Is Unclear.
Trust, But Verify.

181.

What's The Difference
Between *Just Okay* And *Great?*
Your Team Needs To Know!

182.

A Timely Assist
That Helps Someone Get Unstuck
Build Much Loyalty.

183.

When Delegating
Ask Your Staff To Give Updates
Before You'll Need Them.

184.

"I Messed Things Up, Boss."
How You Respond To Those Words
Tells Its Own Story.

185.

Delegation Is
The Art Of Getting Things Done
By *Not* Doing Them.

186.

Some Sudden Bad News.
It's Time To Rally The Troops.
It's Time For Your Best.

187.

Your Reputation
As A Leader Of Others
Will Outlast Your Stay.

188.

Boredom And Fatigue
Can Undermine Any Team
If You Miss The Signs.

189.

TGIF, Right?!
Just Don't Forget That As Boss
You're A Role Model.

190.

The Endless Demands.
The Relentless "One More Thing."
Show Some Restraint, Boss!

191.

Engaging Others.
Even The 'Difficult' Ones.
THAT Is Leadership.

192.

Dole Out Assignments
So That Employees Can Learn
What They Need To Learn.

193.

Regularly Thank
The People Who Get Things Done.
Acknowledge Their Work.

194.

Want To Be Of Help?
Go Ask Your Direct Reports
What's Bothering Them.

195.

When Staff Does Great Work
Just To Make You Proud Of Them.
THAT Is Leadership.

196.

Some Say, "I Don't Know!"
When "I Haven't Thought It Through,"
Is More Likely True.

197.

Whatever You Do
When No One Is Watching You
Is What They'll Watch.

198.

Your Best Employee -
What Makes Him Or Her So Good?
Ask Others For That.

199.

Be A Role Model.
Not Just When Things Go Smoothly.
But When They Don't, Too.

200.

'A' Players Are Great.
But Your 'B' And 'C' Players
Will Drive Your Success.

201.

Best Of Intentions.
Worst Of Possible Outcomes.
What's Your Next Move, Boss?!

202.

Build Capacity.
Not Just *Your* Capacity.
But Your Team's, As Well.

203.

Whatever They Say
Don't Let Their Tone Unnerve You.
Listen Beyond That.

204.

Creative Thinking
Doesn't Seek Just One Answer.
It Looks For Many.

205.

Fun, Friendly, Chats, And
Difficult Conversations
Are All Important.

206.

Helping Your Staff To
Prepare For That Big Meeting.
THAT Is Leadership.

207.

How Do You Signal
You Are More Interested
In Bigger Ideas?

208.

How Much Complaining
Are You Willing To Accept?
End Chats Before That.

209.

Leaders Talk About
The Good Things Happening, Plus
What Needs To Be Said.

210.

It's Regrettable
That Employees Get So Stressed.
Do Something To Help.

211.

Sometimes It's "Sooner!"
Sometimes It's "Not So Fast, There."
You Call The Tempo.

212.

Stay Open Minded.
Allow For Different Methods.
It's Not About You.

213.

Some Choose Diving In.
Others Prefer Wading In.
Their Styles Are Your Tools.

214.

Be There For Your Team
In Victory And Defeat.
They'll Respect You More.

215.

Challenge Your Staff To
Apply More Business Rigor
To All Their Requests

216.

Instead Of Asking
"Why Did You Do What You Did?"
Ask "What Did You Learn?"

MANAGING ACROSS

217.

As You, They're Busy.
As You, They've Got Tight Deadlines.
Peers Deserve Respect.

218.

Always Consider
The Unintended Meaning
Of All That You Say.

219.

Each Conversation
Can Build Your Relationships
Or Dismantle Them.

220.

If How They View You
Differs From Your Own Self-View
There's Work To Be Done.

221.

Subjectivity:
When What You Say And I Say
Are Both Same...And Not.

222.

Collaboration:
It's Not Convincing Others,
But Creating With.

223.

A Leader Knows That
Sharing Information Builds
Stronger Relationships.

224.

Ever Cause A Mess?
Who Rallied To Your Support?
Return The Favor.

225.

Grace In Victory
And Grace In Defeat, As Well.
The High Road, Always.

226.

Not Sure What To Do?
Weigh The Implications Of
Not Doing Each Thing.

227.

Peer Conversations
Can Be Heard In The Moment
And Afterwards, Too.

228.

Opinions Matter.
But They're Far Less Compelling
When Facts Are Ignored.

229.

Opportunity.
Sometimes It Knocks Quite Loudly.
Mostly, It Whispers.

230.

Talking With Others
Should Never Be Confused With
Just Talking At Them.

231.

What Conversations
Could You Be Having Right Now
If You'd Let Yourself?

232.

When Peers Mess Things Up
Frustration Is Natural
But It's Not What's Best.

233.

Patience Is Tricky.
Not Enough Creates *Ill-Will*.
Too Much Creates *Still*.

234.

When You Burn Bridges
You Unnecessarily
Complicate Your World.

235.

Who Listens To You?
What Do They Hear That Others
Seemingly Do Not?

236.

Wondering Aloud
Stimulates Conversations
That Want To Happen.

237.

Your Thought Leadership
Is About Your Ideas, And
Your Response To Theirs.

238.

Respect And Regard:
Foundational Principles
Of All True Leaders.

239.

What You Fault Them For
Is Likely Something You Don't
Like About Yourself.

240.

The Choices We Make
Are Often Undermined By
Preconceived Ideas.

241.

Strengthen Relations
Even When You Don't Have To
So You Won't Have To.

242.

Do Not Problem-Solve
Until You Can Crisply State
What The Problem Is.

243.

How Available
Is Your Attention To Those
Who Say They Need It?

244.

Build Lasting Bridges.
You Just Might Find You Need To
Pass This Way Again.

245.

Open-Mindedness:
It's Not What You Think It Is
If You Disagree.

246.

Who Do You Inspire?
Who Is It That Inspires You?
Spend More Time With Them.

247.

Check Your Messages.
Who's Wanting To Talk With You?
Call Them Back, Quickly.

248.

Many Great Ideas
Start With One Person's Thinking.
Others Then Refine.

249.

Working *Through* Others.
Not Like A Rock Thrown Through Glass
But Health Through Fitness.

250.

How Is Your Rapport
With Your Peers and Your Colleagues?
What Would Improve It?

251.

Basic Common Sense
Is Sometimes All That's Needed.
Often, That's The Case.

252.

Be Approachable.
Develop A Warm Rapport.
You'll Learn So Much More.

253.

Executive Clout
Stems Far Less From Self-ish-ness
Than From Self-less-ness.

254.

Don't Rush To Think That
Just Because No One Speaks Up
Consensus Exists.

255.

How You Contribute
Is Defined By What You Say.
And What You Do Not.

256.

Knowing What You Know.
Knowing What They Need To Know.
Go Connect The Dots.

257.

Let Others Save Face
And They Will Likely Help You,
When You Need It Most.

258.

Look And See Nothing.
Look Again And See Nothing.
Look Again And See.

259.

Misunderstandings:
Focus On Resolving Them,
Early and Often.

260.

More And More Meetings.
Priorities Changing Fast.
Don't Lose Perspective.

261.

Respect And Regard
Creates An Ease And Rapport
That Cannot Be Faked.

262.

There Is Your Message
And Your Message's Timing.
Both Are Important.

263.

Underestimate
The Importance Of Others
At Your Own Peril.

264.

What They Mean To Say
Isn't Always What They Say.
Know The Difference.

265.

What You Say And Do
After It's All Said And Done
Really Matters, Too.

266.

When You're In Conflict
Keep Focused On The Issues
Not The Emotions.

267.

What Conversations
Could You Have, That You *Don't* Have
That You *Ought* To Have?

268.

What Conversations
Could They Be Having With *You*
If You Just Let Them?

269.

Some Times The Best Route
Is Circuitous, That Is,
Collaborative.

270.

When Affecting Change
Help People Understand How
It Benefits *Them.*

271.

When Someone Falters
Do You Help Them Clean Things Up?
Or Just Criticize?

272.

Articulate Both
The 'What' You Want And The 'Why.'
Share Your Rationale.

273.

Others Will Notice
And Talk About What You Do
As What You Don't Do.

274.

Do Not Assume That
Things Will Go As Planned; Prepare
For When They Might Not.

275.

Let Peers Challenge You.
They Will Enjoy The Debate.
You'll Gain Their Support.

276.

What Makes You Follow?
What Makes You Gladly Follow?
Share That With Your Peers.

277.

Feedback From Your Peers
Is Like A Flower's Pollen.
Are You Allergic?!

278.

Getting What You Need
More Quickly Than On Your Own
THAT Is Leadership.

279.

Who You Know Matters.
But Who Knows You Matters More.
Who Needs To Know You?

280.

A Conversation
Can Turn "No, I Did Not Know"
Into "Oh, I See."

281.

Ask For What You Need.
Ask For What They Have To Say.
Then Listen. Listen.

282.

Be Iterative.
Learn From Your Wins And Losses.
Surely. Steadily.

283.

Collaboration
Is Finding A Common Ground
From Which To Advance.

284.

Camaraderie
Is More Than Just Pretending.
It's Truly Caring.

285.

Conflicts Are Less So
When You Stay In The Moment
And Don't Lose Your Cool.

286.

Half-Baked Messaging
Like Some Old Jigsaw Puzzles
Have Missing Pieces.

287.

Help Improve The Mood
Whether It Belongs To You
Or One Of Your Peers.

288.

I Do Not Know You.
I Would Like To Know You, Though.
At Least I Hope So.

289.

Lackluster Questions
Beget Lackluster Answers.
Upgrade Your Questions.

290.

Might It Now Be Time
To Reconsider Ideas
Already Offered?

291.

Not Every Idea
Is A Guaranteed Winner.
Or A Total Waste.

292.

One Conversation
Can Morph "Okay" Into "WOW!!!!"
Go Talk With Someone.

293.

Share Your Big Concerns.
Enlist Their Help and Support.
Together, As One.

294.

The Best Networkers
Don't Only Contact Others.
Others Contact Them.

295.

The Choices You Make
Have Many Implications.
Intended And Not.

296.

When Bad News To Give,
Don't Just Shoot Off An Email.
Tell Them In Person.

297.

Triggered By This One?
Hot Buttons Pushed By That One?
Claim Your Inner Calm.

298.

Two Sides Of A Coin:
Curious And Judgmental.
Which Side Are *You* On?

299.

What Do You Believe?
What Facts Support That Belief?
Who Needs To Hear Them?

300.

What You Have To Say
And How They Have To Hear It.
Both Are Important.

301.

What You Talk About
And How You Talk About It
Reveals Your True Self.

302.

When Working With Peers,
Focus More On Brainstorming
Than Who Said What First.

303.

When Working With Peers
Sometimes You Have To Insist
That They Play Nicely.

304.

When You're Running Late
Call Ahead To Let Them Know.
Don't Assume They'll Know.

305.

Wondering Aloud
Is What Helps Brainstorming Work.
Ideas Spawn Ideas.

306.

It's Not About You.
It's About What You Can Do
To Help *Others* Do.

307.

Do Not Judge Them So.
Strive To Understand, Instead.
And Then Build From There.

308.

Who Knows Your True North?
Empower Them To Tell You
When You Are Off Course.

309.

Enjoy Good Debate
For The Challenge It Provides
To Articulate.

310.

Who *Pings* You For Help?
What Makes You Valuable?
If You're Not Sure, Ask.

311.

Whose Idea Was That?
Give Credit Where It's Due.
And To Whom It's Due.

312.

Peers Who Believe That
Sarcasm Is Respectful
Are Missing The Point.

313.

Helping One's Colleagues
Tends To Be A Forgotten
Part Of Leadership.

314.

Problems Are Not Bad.
They Are Just New Assignments
For Us To Address.

315.

Staying Connected
With Helpful People You've Met
Is A Good Idea.

316.

You See What They Don't.
But If You Help Them See It
Everyone Will See.

317.

Reasonableness:
One More Way To Demonstrate
'Respect For Your Peers.'

318.

Ideas Are Like Dough.
They Grow When They are Kneaded.
As When They're Needed.

319.

Who Ups Your Game More?
Those Most Critical Of You?
Or Your Biggest Fans?

320.

What Moves The Needle?
How Can You Have More Impact
On *Business* Results?

321.

Reach Out To Someone.
Go Explore Beyond Your Clique.
Go Cross-Pollinate.

322.

Others' Opinions:
What They May Think About You.
And What They Do Not.

323.

Don't Just Assume That
Just Because You Understand,
They Understand, Too.

324.

Clarification:
Turning What You Said
Into What You Meant.

MANAGING WITHIN

325.

What's Holding You Back?
Is It That Powerful That
You'll Let It Stop You?

326.

Opportunity:
What Problems Can Turn Into
If We Allow Them.

327.

A Leader's Choices
Are Less Between Right And Wrong
Than Right Versus Right.

328.

Comfort In Sameness
Too Easily Morphs Into
Boredom And Fatigue.

329.

Perfectionism:
The Habit Of You Taking
Too Much Time On Things.

330.

Each Day Is A Chance
To Build On Yesterday Or
Start Over Again.

331.

Procrastination:
A Luxury You Don't Have.
Time Is A-Wasting.

332.

Decision-Making
Deciding What TO Decide
And What NOT To, Too.

333.

Fight Against Staleness.
It's Bad For Potato Chips.
It's Bad For Your Mind.

334.

How Do You Recharge?
By Yourself? Or With Others?
Do What You Prefer.

335.

How Do You Worry?
In A Way That Distracts You?
Or Focuses You?

336.

If Work Feels Like Work
Shift Your Focus From What's *Hard*
To What's *Important.*

337.

Is Time The Problem?
Or The Choices You Must Make
Vis-à-Vis The Time?

338.

It's All About You.
Then, Again, It's Really Not.
Such A Paradox.

339.

It's Not About Fear.
It's What You Do With The Fear
That Really Matters.

340.

Managing *Yourself*
Can Be The Biggest Challenge
You Ever Attempt.

341.

Professional Growth
Is Measured By Its Absence
More Than Its Presence.

342.

Sometimes The Best Thing
Is To Get Up From Your Desk
And Go Take A Walk.

343.

Sphere Of Influence:
The Reason Why What You Do
Affects More Than You.

344.

Stop Kidding Yourself.
Time Management Is Not It.
Self-Management Is.

345.

Respect Has Two Parts.
How You Treat Other People;
How You Treat Yourself.

346.

The 'U' In "Struggle"
Prompts A Question Worth Asking:
"How Can 'U' Change That?"

347.

The Act Of Thinking
May Not Seem So Powerful,
But Its Impact Is.

348.

The Way You Behave
When Things Are Not Going Right.
THAT Is Leadership.

349.

Want To Up Your Game?
Learn To Make Tough Decisions.
Don't Just 'Solve' Problems.

350.

Watch What's Happening.
Listen To What's Happening.
Make Something Happen.

351.

What A Peaceful Dream.
Everything Going As Planned.
Clearly, 'Twas A Dream!

352.

What All You *Can* Do
Is Far Less Important Than
All That You *Do* Do!

353.

What Are You Learning?
And What Do You Need To Learn?
Don't Confuse The Two.

354.

Starting Strong Is Key.
So Is Keeping Things Going.
As Is Finishing.

355.

What Do You Avoid
That You Probably Shouldn't?
And When Will That End?!

356.

What Do You Not Know
That You Know You Need To Know
In Order To Know?

357.

What Are Your Limits?
How Do You Test Them To See
If They've Changed Any?

358.

What Helps You More?
The Power Of An Idea?
Or Someone Helping?

359.

Whatever Your Strengths,
If Your Weaknesses Guide You,
You Will Lose Your Way.

360.

What's Easy For You
Some Will Find Impossible.
And Vice Versa, Too.

361.

What Is Confidence?
It's Helping Others See You
At Your Very Best.

362.

Whatever You Do
Do The Next Thing That You Do
The Best That You Can.

363.

When Setbacks Happen
How Long 'Til You Recover?
What Would Speed That Up?

364.

When We Face Our Fears
Sometimes We're Frightened To Death.
But Often We're Not.

365.

When You Keep Doing
The Way You've Always Done Things
You Can't Call That 'Growth.'

366.

Why Does The First Step
Always Seem More Difficult
Before, Than After?!

367.

Wisdom Is Knowing
What You Need To Do When You
Don't Know What To Do.

368.

With The Right Mindset
Even A Big Mess Is An
Opportunity.

369.

Your Leadership Style
Can Be Described In Three Words.
Which Ones Describe You?

370.

Whatever Your Skills
Learn How To Utilize Them
To Solve Big Problems.

371.

Ever Wonder Why
We Can Get So Much More Done
When We Don't Have Time?!

372.

Opportunities:
Whatever You Might Do With
Whatever Appears.

373.

Some Days Are Easy.
But They Pay You What They Do
For The *Other* Days.

374.

Learning Separates
Leaders From Everyone Else.
What Are You Learning?

375.

All You Want To Do
And All That You Need To Do
Rarely Overlap.

376.

"I Have It Somewhere,"
Is Not A Filing System.
Go Clean Up That Mess!

377.

A Leader's Workweek
Is Less Defined By The Days
Than Priorities.

378.

If You're Unprepared
The Stress Will Seem Much Greater
Than If You're Ready.

379.

Don't Rush Just To Rush.
Leaders Know When To Hurry
And When To Go Slow.

380.

Every Leap Of Faith,
Whether It Pays Off Or Not
Shows Your Character.

381.

Creativity
Is Not Just Building From Scratch,
But With What You Have.

382.

Gathering Info:
The Art Of Asking Questions
That Gather Info.

383.

How Do You Re-Charge?
Do You Race To Somewhere New?
Or Do You Slow Down?

384.

A Cluttered Mind Is
Much Worse Than A Cluttered Desk.
But Neither Is Good.

385.

Knowing What You Need
And Knowing How To Get It.
THAT Is Leadership.

386.

That You Tried And Failed
Is More About You Trying
Than Not Succeeding.

387.

No Matter The Job
There'll Be Noise And Distraction.
Have A Plan For It.

388.

Poor Work Done On Time
Shows Respect For The Due Date,
But Not For Yourself.

389.

Our Limitations
May *Seem* Indisputable,
But Really They're Not.

390.

Taking Care Of Things
Before They Become Urgent.
THAT Is Leadership.

391.

The Best Decisions
Serve Multiple Purposes
With A Single Stroke.

392.

The Question To Ask
To Help You Figure Things Out
Is "What *Don't* I Know?"

393.

Two Sides Of A Coin:
Confidence And Arrogance.
Which Side Are *You* On?

394.

We All Have Self-Doubts.
Leaders Just Turn Theirs Into
Actionable Steps.

395.

What Are You Doing
To Sharpen Your Learning Edge?
It Dulls With Disuse.

396.

What Looks Like A Mess
May Or May Not Be A Mess.
Perceptions Matter.

397.

What Motivates You?
What Sustains Your Attention?
Know. Seek. Find. Embrace.

398.

What You Believe Is
Increasingly Important
When You Don't Believe.

399.

What's Crucial About
Leadership Development
Is That You Do It.

400.

What's Next On Your List?
You Don't Have A List, You Say?
You Don't Have A List?!

401.

When Was The Last Time
You Challenged Yourself To Be
Your Absolute Best?

402.

Whenever In Doubt
Remind Yourself Of The Goal
And Proceed From There.

403.

Your Experience
Is A Limited Resource.
Go Learn Something New.

404.

Your Leadership Brand
Is Derived From What You Think
And How You Behave.

405.

Because You're Busy
Things May Fall Between The Cracks.
Don't Let That Happen.

406.

Ends Justify Means?
That's About Leadership And
One's Business Ethics.

407.

Sometimes The Best Plan
Is To Be Open To New
Possibilities.

408.

Curiosity:
That You're Wondering About
What You're Wondering.

409.

Frustration Is Not
A Luxury That Leaders
Can Often Afford.

410.

Imagination
Determines What Could Go Wrong
And How To Fix It.

411.

Staying At Your Best
Sometimes Means Giving Yourself
Some Well-Earned Time Off.

412.

Strategic Thinking
Focuses On What's Missing
As Much As What's Not.

413.

Embrace The Challenge
No Matter How Large Or Small.
It Helps With The Stress.

414.

Eventually,
It Will Always Come Down To
How You Treat People.

415.

Make Things As Simple
As They Can Possibly Be,
But No More Simple.

416.

That You Doubt Yourself
Matters Less Than What You Do
When You *Are* In Doubt.

417.

It's Often Stressful
Being The Person In Charge.
Take Care Of Yourself.

418.

Time Passes Quickly.
Although Sometimes It Does Not.
Funny How That Is.

419.

Stretch Your Comfort Zone
So That You Can Stretch Yourself
With Far Greater Ease.

420.

Powerful Leaders
Harnessing Abilities.
Their Own And Others.

421.

Change Is What Lets Us
Leave Behind The Things That We
Never Much Cared For.

422.

Are You Clear On What
Unintended Outcomes Your
Decision Might Cause?

423.

Is It A Problem
Or An Opportunity
That Motivates More?

424.

Control What You Can.
Embrace All That You Cannot.
Commit, Regardless.

ABOUT THE AUTHOR

As Founder of LeadershipTraction®, a leadership development consultancy, Barry Zweibel ("zwy-BELL") likes to say that he 'pokes and prods' his clients to become better leaders. They like to say that he coaches and mentors them to:

- Think more strategically, more of the time
- Collaborate more fully and freely
- Connect more deeply with their personal power, presence, and place, and
- Routinely deliver more truly game-changing results

Barry's insights on leadership, coaching, mentoring, conflict management, and career acceleration have been widely published in both online and in-print media. *The Wall Street Journal* and *CNN.com* have quoted him as a subject matter expert.

The International Coach Federation recognizes Barry as a *Master Certified Coach* – the 'Gold Standard' of coach credentialing – a distinction that fewer than 2% of all coaches, worldwide, have achieved. He is also a highly regarded speaker, instructor, facilitator, and thought-leader, and has created and taught curriculum at both the corporate and collegiate levels.

Barry lives, with his wife, in the Chicagoland area.

NOTES

NOTES

NOTES